DESIGNS IN SCIENCE
WATER

SALLY and ADRIAN MORGAN

Evans

EVANS BROTHERS LIMITED

Evans Brothers Limited
2A Portman Mansions
Chiltern Street
London W1M 1LE

©Evans Brothers Limited 1994

First published 1994

Printed by Wing King Tong Co Ltd.

ISBN 0 237 51426 5

Managing Editor: Su Swallow
Editors: Catherine Bradley and Kate Scarborough
Designer: Neil Sayer
Production: Jenny Mulvanny
Illustrations: Hardlines, Charlbury
David McAllister

Acknowledgements

For permission to reproduce copyright material the authors and publishers gratefully acknowledge the following:

Cover Ronald Toms, Oxford Scientific Films
Title page Hank de Lespinasse, The Image Bank
Contents page Sally Morgan, Ecoscene **page 4** European Space Agency, Eumetsat, Science Photo Library **page 5** (top) Robert Harding Picture Library (bottom) Harold Taylor, Oxford Scientific Films **page 6** Tim Shepherd, Oxford Scientific Films **page 7** (left) Jeff Foott Productions, Bruce Coleman Ltd (right) Martin Dohrn, Science Photo Library **page 8** (top) Leroy Grannis, Planet Earth Pictures (middle top) John Bracegirdle, Planet Earth Pictures (middle bottom) Glover, Ecoscene (bottom) Jules Cowan, Bruce Coleman Ltd **page 9** Dr George Gornacz, Science Photo Library **page 10** (top) Sally Morgan, Ecoscene (bottom) Alistair MacEwen, Oxford Scientific Films **page 11** Sally Morgan, Ecoscene **page 12** A C Waltham, Robert Harding Picture Library **page 13** (left) Mark N Boulton, Bruce Coleman Ltd (right) Robert Harding Picture Library **page 14** (top) Gryniewicz, Ecoscene (bottom) David Campione, Science Photo Library **page 15** (top) Max Gibbs, Oxford Scientific Films (bottom) Sally Morgan, Ecoscene **page 16** Last Resort Picture Library **page 17** (top) Sally Morgan, Ecoscene (bottom) Ecoscene **page 18** David Spears, Bruce Coleman Ltd **page 19** (top) Last Resort Picture Library (middle) Last Resort Picture Library (bottom) Harold Taylor, Oxford Scientific Films **page 20** (top) Sally Morgan, Ecoscene (bottom)

Adam Hart-Davis, Science Photo Library **page 21** (top) Peter Hendrie, The Image Bank (bottom) Barrie Rokeach, The Image Bank **page 22** (left) Brown, Ecoscene (right) David Austen, Bruce Coleman Ltd **page 23** (top) Mark Conlin, Planet Earth Pictures (middle) Caney, Ecoscene (bottom) Bard Martin, The Image Bank **page 24** Brown, Ecoscene **page 25** Sally Morgan, Ecoscene **page 26** (top) Kim Taylor, Bruce Coleman Ltd (bottom) Tom McHugh, Photo Researchers Ltd, Oxford Scientific Films **page 27** (top) Francois Gohier, Photo Researchers Inc, Oxford Scientific Films (bottom) John Lythgoe, Planet Earth Pictures **page 28** (top) Ronald Toms, Oxford Scientific Films (bottom) Kloske, Ecoscene **page 29** (top) Jane Gifford, NHPA (bottom) Maurice Harvey, The Hutchison Library **page 30** (top) Mary Clay, Planet Earth Pictures (bottom) Will McIntyre, Science Photo Library **page 31** Isaac Kehimar, Oxford Scientific Films **page 32** (top) Don Morley (bottom) Sally Morgan, Ecoscene **page 33** Peter Menzel, Science Photo Library **page 34** Brian Henderson, Bruce Coleman Ltd **page 35** (top) Wayne Lawler, Ecoscene (bottom) Dr Eckart Pott, Bruce Coleman Ltd **page 36** (top) Sally Morgan, Ecoscene (bottom) John Mead, Science Photo Library **page 37** Sally Morgan, Ecoscene **page 38** Pete Turner, The Image Bank **page 39** (top left) Gryiewicz, Ecoscene (top right) Steve Proehl, The Image Bank (bottom) Sally Morgan, Ecoscene **page 40** Towse, Ecoscene **page 41** Valdimir Lange, The Image Bank **page 42** WWF, IUCN **page 43** (top) Andrew Brown, Ecoscene (bottom) Andrew Brown, Ecoscene

Contents

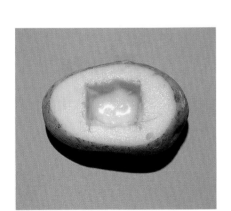

Introduction

If you look at a photograph of our planet taken from space, you can see that a large amount of it is covered by seas and oceans. In fact, more than 70 per cent of the surface is water. The depth of the water varies, but on average it is 3.5 km from the waves at the surface to the sea bed. In some oceans, deep trenches in the sea bed reach almost 11 km into the earth. The incredible quantity of water found in the oceans and the polar ice caps (which are also clearly visible from space) makes it one of the earth's most abundant substances.

The water in the oceans is salt water, that is, water that contains a lot of salts, such as sodium chloride. Water that falls as rain or snow and collects in rivers and lakes is described as fresh water. The main difference between salt and fresh water is the quantity of salts. Even fresh water has a small amount of salt in it. All living beings such as human beings need fresh water, not salt water, in order to survive. There is a very limited supply of fresh water on the earth. Only about one per cent of the water on earth is actually fresh water, and more than 70 per cent of that is locked up in the ice of the Antarctic ice cap.

Much of the earth is covered by water. There is also a lot of water vapour in the atmosphere and droplets of water in the clouds.

Water and life

! *If all the ice in the world was to melt at once, the sea level would rise by more than 60 metres, flooding low-lying areas.*

Without water, life as we know it could not exist. Large bodies of water provide a stable environment since the water can absorb a lot of heat energy without increasing in temperature (see page 9). It is for this reason that life on our planet first evolved in water. The very first life forms appeared more than 3500 million years ago. They were simple, single-celled organisms such as bacteria and algae. Even today, the oceans are still full of these single-celled organisms drifting gently in the ocean currents. They are known collectively as plankton.

The huge variety of plants and animals that we know today evolved from these first simple organisms. Many of these animals went on to colonise the land where, unlike life in the sea, life is restricted to a relatively narrow band above and below the surface of the land itself. Eventually, some air-breathing mammals returned to the sea, and evolved into whales and dolphins.

Water is a habitat for many organisms, and it also forms an essential part of living cells. For example, while the human body is made up of many different substances, including carbohydrates, fats and proteins, more than 68 per cent of our body weight is water. In some organisms such as sea anemones and jelly fish this percentage is even higher.

! *A human being can survive 60 days or more without food, but less than 60 hours without water.*

Ice is frozen water. Only a small amount of the iceberg appears above the surface of the water. Most of it is submerged.

The body of a teenage boy or girl contains about 35 litres of water.

Measurement

These abbreviations are used in this book.

Units of length
km kilometre
m metre
cm centimetre

Units of mass
kg kilogramme
g gramme

Units of temperature
°C degrees Celsius

Units of area
cm² centimetre squared

Units of volume
l litre
cm³ cubic centimetre

Key words
Water a colourless, odourless liquid made of hydrogen and oxygen.

The surface of the oceans is colonised by tiny animals called zooplankton. Many are the larvae of larger animals.

In this book you will discover the many ways in which water is essential to our survival, see how it is used in our bodies and explore some of its many different uses in industry. We use water every day for drinking, washing, cooking and recreation. Water is used in many industrial processes such as the making of steel, cement, paper and electricity. In the later chapters of this book, you will learn that fresh water is a limited resource that has to be conserved and cleaned so it can be used over and over again.

Important words are explained at the end of each section under the heading of **Key words** and in the glossary on page 44. You will find some amazing facts in each section, together with some experiments and some questions for you to think about.

Water is the most common liquid on the earth. It is estimated that there are 1.5 million million million tonnes of water on earth.

The water molecule

Pure water is a colourless and odourless liquid comprised entirely of one type of molecule. The water molecule has a simple structure. It is made up of two hydrogen atoms and one oxygen atom bonded (joined) together. These bonds are difficult to break once they have been formed. Water has the chemical formula H_2O.

Inside an atom

All substances are made up of atoms. An atom is a tiny structure, far too small to be seen with the naked eye. It consists of a heavy nucleus in the centre, which is surrounded by moving electrons. The nucleus usually contains two types of particle, protons and neutrons. The proton is positively charged, while the neutron is neutral (this means it has no electrical charge). The electrons are very much smaller than protons and they have a negative charge. They move constantly, forming an orbiting cloud around the nucleus. There are usually an equal number of electrons and protons in an atom so that the negative and positive charges balance each other out.

Water is made from hydrogen and oxygen atoms. The hydrogen atom is the smallest known atom, with just one proton and one electron. It does not contain any neutrons. The oxygen atom is much larger than the hydrogen atom and has eight protons, eight electrons and eight neutrons.

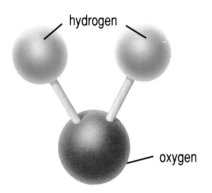

hydrogen

oxygen

The water molecule is made up of two atoms of hydrogen and one of oxygen. Oxygen is a much bigger atom than hydrogen.

Three states of matter

At temperatures of 0°C, water turns into its solid form. Ice is made up of crystals.

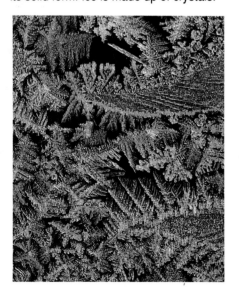

Any substance can exist in any one of three states, gas, liquid or solid. The earth is the only planet in this solar system that has the right conditions for water to exist in all three states. However, water most commonly exists in the liquid state. In a liquid, the molecules are free to move around, but they are still attracted to one another and cling together. This allows a liquid to change shape easily and to flow. At 0°C, the freezing point of water, water changes state from a liquid to a solid, which we know as ice. The molecules within a crystal of ice are bonded together and cannot move around one another. This gives the crystals of ice a firm shape. If the ice is given heat energy, however, the molecules within the ice crystal begin to vibrate. Eventually they will break free from the fixed bonds to become water again. If even more heat energy is supplied, the water molecules will vibrate so fast that some will break free of the liquid attraction. These molecules evaporate from the surface of the liquid to form a gas, known as water vapour. These changes

This geyser is a natural spring that discharges a column of boiling water and steam. People have to heat water to its boiling point of 100°C to get steam, or water vapour.

What are the best conditions for drying clothes on a washing line?

At one point during the Pleistocene Ice Age more than 30 per cent of the earth's surface was covered by ice.

of state are reversible. Water vapour can turn back into a liquid by a process called condensation, while liquid water can freeze to form the solid ice.

Water, like any liquid, can evaporate at almost any temperature above its freezing point. For example, washing can be hung outside on a cold day and yet water will still evaporate from the surface of the clothes. The boiling point of a liquid is the highest temperature the liquid can reach without evaporating completely. The boiling point of water is 100°C. The molecules of water in water vapour have a lot of energy and they move freely, filling any available space. If water vapour is cooled, it will lose heat energy. The water vapour molecules will move more slowly and will condense and become liquid again.

In the following chapters, the term water refers to water in its liquid state.

The water cycle

Although the supplies of fresh water on earth are limited compared to the volume of salt water, it is not likely that we will ever actually run out of water. The reason for this is that water is recycled naturally. The complete process is known as the water cycle.

1 Heat energy from the sun causes water molecules to evaporate from the surface of oceans, seas, rivers, lakes, and the earth's surface. Water also evaporates from the surface of animals when they sweat or pant, and from the surfaces of the plants in a process called transpiration (see page 19).

2 Water vapour rises and, as it does so, it cools and condenses to form small droplets of water. The water droplets form clouds high in the atmosphere that are moved by currents of air.

3 The droplets cool further and join together to form even larger droplets, which then fall as rain. If the air is very cold, the droplets will fall as hail, sleet or even snow. Rain is particularly heavy on higher land.

4 The rainwater runs off into streams, which join to form rivers. These empty into lakes or oceans. Some of the water will be absorbed by the ground to be used by plants or will seep deep into the ground to reach the water table (see page 22). The water may travel underground along a water-bearing rock layer called an aquifer (see page 21) and eventually reappear from a spring. The water that heads into rivers, lakes and seas will then evaporate and the cycle is repeated.

How do people interfere with the natural water cycle? What are the consequences of this interference?

The pictures, from top to bottom, show four different stages in the water cycle:
1 evaporation
2 condensation
3 rainfall
4 river formation followed by evaporation

What makes water so special?

The oceans absorb a lot of heat energy. This means that water is an ideal environment for animals such as fish which cannot regulate their own body temperatures.

Water is a very unusual and extremely useful substance. For a start, it has a high heat capacity. This means that water is able to absorb a lot of heat energy without becoming very much warmer: the temperature will only rise very slowly. Once the water is warm, however, it will lose heat very slowly. In deep oceans, the temperature remains relatively constant at about 4°C, thereby providing a very stable environment for marine plants and animals.

Water's heat capacity means that it also takes a lot of heat energy to cause water molecules to evaporate. Most lakes rarely dry up in very hot weather because water can absorb a large amount of heat energy without becoming hot enough to lose a lot of water by evaporation.

It is the absorption of huge amounts of energy that creates currents in the seas and oceans. Waters around the equator absorb a lot of heat energy from the sun. The warmer water is less dense than cold water. This is because the molecules in warm water are moving rapidly and are spread out so there are fewer of them in a given volume compared to cooler water. Therefore the warm water rises to the surface and (in the northern hemisphere) it forms a current moving north towards cooler water. The cooler waters of the more northern parts of the hemisphere sink because they are dense and flow back towards the equator. These movements of warm and cold water create massive circulating currents in the ocean that are largely responsible for the global climate.

! *Water in the Gulf Stream flows at speeds of up to 225 km per day.*

The map shows the water currents circulating around the world. Warm currents give places such as Japan, Great Britain and Alaska less severe winters than other northern areas that lack a warm current, allowing people to survive more comfortably in these northern latitudes.

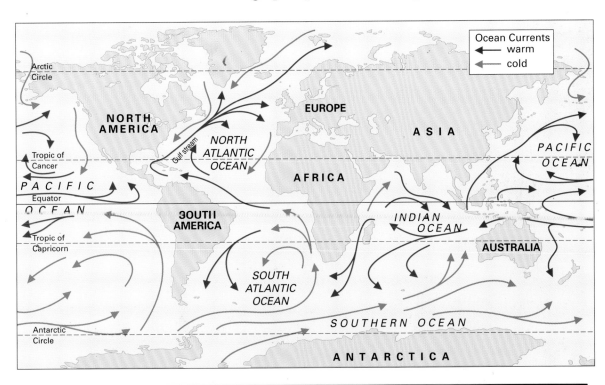

A layer of ice floats on the top of a pond.

If a pond was covered by ice where would you find the warmest layer of water?

Why does only one fifth of an iceberg float above the surface of the water?

This pond skater is supported on the surface of the water by surface tension.

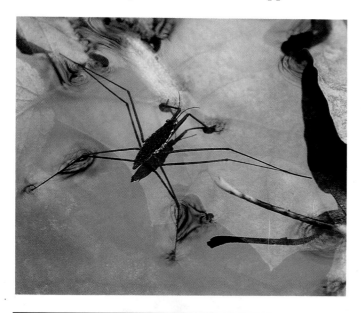

One of the most amazing features of water is that it is less dense in its solid state than in its liquid state. This is evident when we see ice cubes floating in water, or a coating of ice on a pond or an iceberg floating in the sea. When water freezes, a lot of air is incorporated into the solid structure, increasing its volume. The increase in volume reduces its density, allowing it to float. This expansion of volume when water freezes can be dangerous if the water is inside a container, such as a pipe or a plant cell wall, as the expansion can cause the pipe or cell wall to split open. As the temperature rises above freezing point the ice melts and the water leaks from the broken pipe or drains from the damaged cell.

A layer of ice can sometimes provide a protective barrier. Some plants and animals living in ponds survive cold winters because, when the top layer of water freezes, a layer of ice is formed. This acts as an insulator against even colder weather. Animals survive in the bottom of the pond, because the water there stays at a temperature of 4°C.

Many pond animals also make use of another property of water, surface tension. If you carefully touch the top of a volume of water, there may appear to be a thin skin over the surface of the water. This 'skin' is caused by surface tension. It is quite strong, strong enough for small animals, such as pond skaters, to be supported and to move with ease across the surface of water.

Surface tension occurs because water molecules are attracted to one another and so tend to stick together. At the water's surface they are attracted to each other more strongly than to air molecules, which means that any molecule rising above its neighbours tends to be drawn back downwards again. The result is an apparent skin on the surface of the water. However, if you look carefully at water in a clear glass, you may notice that, where the glass meets the water, the water is trying to 'creep' up the sides. This is due to a strong attraction between water molecules and the molecules in the glass.

Water is unusual in that its surface tension is much higher than expected in liquid, in fact almost three times higher.

Preventing ice formation

Water can be prevented from freezing by the addition of various chemicals. Salt, for example, lowers the temperature at which water freezes to several degrees below 0°C. Salt is often spread on roads during cold weather to prevent ice from forming. A chemical called ethylene glycol, or antifreeze, is put in car radiators to stop the water in the radiator from freezing. A solution containing 33 per cent ethylene glycol and 66 per cent water will have a freezing point of -20°C.

Some plants and animals use chemicals to prevent cell damage when they are exposed to temperatures below 0°C. The Siberian salamander (an animal resembling a newt) can survive temperatures as low as -50°C. The summer in Siberia only lasts for three to four months, so for the rest of the year the salamander survives frozen in the soil or vegetation. In late summer it starts to adapt to the falling temperatures by producing antifreeze chemicals that replace the water in its blood and protect the cells from ice crystals. Other animals can survive being frozen too. Most frogs can hibernate under rocks, or in the water under ice with up to 65 per cent of the water in their body as ice.

Many animals living in icy waters, for example fish living in the Arctic, have special protein molecules in their blood and body fluids, called antifreeze proteins. However, these proteins do not act like the antifreeze in a car, lowering the freezing point of water. Instead, they cover any ice crystal immediately it forms and prevent it from growing in the body and damaging its cells. Recent tests have shown that antifreeze proteins may become very

! *Siberian salamanders can remain frozen in the ground for many years and when thawed, resume life as if nothing had happened.*

EXPERIMENT

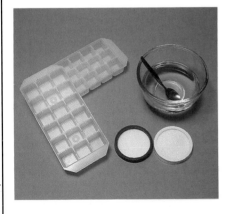

Freezing points

In this simple experiment you will discover the effect of common salt on the freezing point of water. You will need two plastic ice cube trays, salt, sugar, a teaspoon, a small bowl, a stop watch or clock and some cold water.

1 Fill one of the ice cube trays with tap water. Place the tray in the freezer.

2 Record the time it takes for the water in the tray to freeze completely.

3 Half-fill the small bowl with water and add one heaped teaspoon of salt. Stir the water thoroughly to dissolve the salt. Fill the second ice cube tray with the salt water.

4 Record the time it takes for the salt water to freeze. Does the salt water freeze at all?

5 Repeat the experiment, but this time dissolve sugar in the water instead of salt. How long does it take to freeze? Does sugar have any effect on the freezing point of water?

How does the formation of ice in cells damage living organisms?

important in the future. They may be used in the food industry, for example to control the formation of ice crystals in ice cream; they may also be used to preserve human tissue. Genetic engineers are experimenting with plants, especially crops, to help them create their own antifreeze proteins to make them frost resistant.

Acid rain

A snail called the date shell is able to bore holes in limestone by dissolving the rock with acid produced by its body.

Normally, water is neither acid nor alkaline: it has a neutral pH of 7. The pH scale is a measure of the acidity or alkalinity of a substance, and ranges from 1 (very acidic) to 14 (very alkaline). However, chemical substances can dissolve in water to make it acidic or alkaline. For example, sulphur dioxide, a gas that is produced in the natural world, dissolves readily in water to make it acidic. Water can also become acidic if it flows through acidic rocks such as granite or it can become alkaline if it flows through calcium-rich rocks such as chalk or limestone.

Acid water is responsible for the vast underground caves found in many limestone areas. As the acid water slowly filters through the cracks in the limestone, a chemical reaction breaks down the rock. The limestone is rich in calcium carbonate, and it reacts with the acid. As it does so, the rock becomes much weaker and crumbles away. Over thousands of years, this erosion has caused, and is still causing, the formation of enormous caves and underground tunnel systems.

The same process is now occurring because of environmental pollution. The burning of fossil fuels in power stations and in cars causes the formation of sulphur dioxide gas. This gas rises up into

Underground cave systems are created when acid water moves through limestone.

The trees and plants in this forest are surrounded by acid fog, which damages them and prevents new growth.

So much of this stone statue has been eroded by acid rain that parts of it have been broken away.

Key words
Evaporation a change in state from liquid to gas.
Heat capacity the amount of heat energy required to raise the temperature of a certain amount of water by 1°C.
Surface tension a molecular force that pulls the surface of a liquid into the smallest possible area.

the atmosphere where it dissolves in water vapour to form weak sulphuric acid. When this acid water vapour condenses and falls to the ground, it is known as acid rain. Acid rain can have a devastating effect on trees and lakes, especially in high areas which experience heavy rainfall. The acid rain falling on forests gradually changes the pH level of the soil, in turn affecting the health of the trees. Conifer trees are particularly susceptible to acid rain. Over a period of time, their needles turn yellow and drop off. Within a few years the damage to the needles is sufficient to cause the trees to die.

When acidic water drains into lakes, it affects the pH of the lake water. Acid water damages the gills of fish such as trout and salmon. Small invertebrate animals in the lakes will also die and in time the lakes will become lifeless. Acid rain damage is very common in Scandinavia, Eastern Europe and parts of North America. Much of the acid rain has been produced from industrial nations far from these areas, but the prevailing winds carry the acid rain over great distances. Acid rain also affects buildings made of limestone, such as churches and cathedrals. The acid rain damages the surface of statues and intricate stonework. Eventually all of the detail on the stone is worn away. The problem is difficult to solve completely, but increased use of special filters on industrial chimneys does help to reduce the amount of sulphur dioxide getting into the atmosphere.

Water as a solvent

So much sucrose is transported down the stem of the sugar cane that it is a major source of sugar for people. The sap from sugar cane is heated to evaporate the water, leaving crystals of sugar.

Many substances dissolve in water. A substance that dissolves in a liquid is said to be soluble. Sugar, for example, is soluble in water. Water is the solvent and sugar is known as the solute. The solvent and the solute together form a solution. When water is the solvent, the solution is said to be an aqueous solution. Since there is so much water in living organisms (see page 4), water is a very important solvent. Substances such as glucose dissolve in the water of the blood, which allows it to be carried around the human body (see page 18). In plants, the most commonly transported substance is sucrose, which is also soluble in water.

There is a limit to the amount of solute that can be dissolved in a solvent. For example, if increasing amounts of sugar are added to water there will come a point at which no more sugar will dissolve in the water. The solution is then said to be saturated. The point at which saturation is reached depends on the temperature of the solvent, because warm water will dissolve more sugar than cold water. There is an important exception to this general rule. Gases can dissolve in liquids. However, gases actually become less soluble as the temperature rises. Water will hold more dissolved oxygen at a low temperature than it will at a high temperature. This has an important effect on the living organisms found in water. Fish such as salmon and trout need a lot of oxygen and are very sensitive to the amount of oxygen dissolved

Fish require a lot of oxygen so they are usually the first animals to die if oxygen levels in the water fall.

? *Can you think of five substances found in the home that are soluble in water?*

in the water. One particular type of water pollution, thermal pollution, can have a dramatic effect on these fish. Power stations use water from rivers and seas as a coolant (see page 32) and return it to the source as warmer water. However, the warmer water contains less oxygen, so salmon and trout often die when hot water is pumped into their river.

The same thing can sometimes happen during hot weather when the temperature of the water in the river becomes unusually high. There is little that can be done to reduce the water temperature, but it is possible to raise the oxygen level artificially. In parts of the River Thames, and in a few other rivers, a boat called a bubbler travels to problem areas and bubbles oxygen directly into the water. However this only provides a short-term answer.

Sometimes it is possible to make more of a substance dissolve in water without raising the temperature. One method of achieving this is to increase the pressure being applied to the liquid. If a force is applied to a liquid, more gas

The oxygen content of the water in fish tanks can be raised by pumping air directly into the water.

EXPERIMENT

Saturated solutions

In this simple experiment you will discover how much solute can be dissolved into a certain volume of water. You will compare the solubility of two substances at two different temperatures. You will need a large beaker or container, a thermometer, a measuring jug, some weighing scales, a spoon, some cold water, some warm water, a little common salt (sodium chloride) and some sugar.

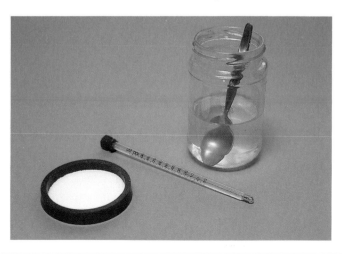

1 Pour 100 cm³ of cold water into the beaker. Take the temperature of the water. Weigh out 10 g of salt and add it to the water. Stir the solution to help the salt dissolve.

2 Add another 10 g of salt to the water. Does it all dissolve? Keep adding 10 g of salt and stirring until no more salt will dissolve. You now have a saturated solution.

3 Repeat this experiment using water from the hot tap. Ideally the water should have a temperature of approximately 40°C. Note how much salt you have to add until no more will dissolve. Can you dissolve more salt in the warm water?

4 Repeat the whole experiment again using first cold then hot water, but replacing the salt with sugar.

Which is more soluble, salt or sugar? What effect does the temperature of the water have on solubility? You could try this experiment using other substances from the kitchen, such as instant coffee.

Many naturally fizzy mineral waters have the gas removed from them before bottling. The gas is then injected back at a higher pressure than it naturally has, making the water extra fizzy.

molecules will dissolve in the liquid. Fizzy drinks are an example of this technique in action. The bubbles in drinks are made by the gas carbon dioxide, which is dissolved into the drink under pressure. When the can or bottle is opened, the pressure is released and the excess gas is able to escape in the form of bubbles. As the gas bubbles to the surface, the drink loses its fizz. It will eventually become flat. In some places of the world water comes out of the ground already fizzy! The water in the ground is under pressure and contains dissolved gases, such as carbon dioxide. As the water leaves the ground the pressure is reduced, allowing the bubbles of gas to escape into the atmosphere.

Hard and soft water

In many parts of the world a hard, white deposit gradually develops inside kettles, pipes and other water containers. The water in these areas is said to be hard. Another sign of hard water is that it is difficult to get lather from soap and a lot of scum is produced. In soft water areas, only a small amount of soap or shampoo is needed to generate a lot of lather. Hard water contains dissolved calcium and magnesium salts such as calcium hydrogen carbonate (the most common) and magnesium sulphate.

Hard water is usually found in areas where there are limestone or chalk rocks. These rocks are rich in minerals that are insoluble in water. However, if the water is just slightly acidic (see page 12), the calcium carbonate in the rocks reacts with the acid in the water and is converted into calcium hydrogen carbonate. When hard water is boiled, the calcium hydrogen carbonate breaks down into calcium carbonate. Since calcium carbonate is insoluble, it comes out of solution and collects on the sides of the kettle to form a scale or fur. This is known as lime scale. The water that is left in the kettle has now become soft! Hard water containing only calcium hydrogen carbonate is described as being temporarily hard, since boiling will remove the hardness from it. However, if the water contains other calcium and magnesium salts, the hardness cannot be removed by boiling and so it is described as being a permanent hard water.

In the past, a major problem with using soaps in hard water areas was the

The element of this electric kettle is covered in hard white lime scale.

EXPERIMENT

Testing for hard water

In this experiment you will test the hardness of a number of different water samples. You will need first to collect a selection of water samples. Try to collect samples of tap water, water that has been boiled and then cooled, distilled water, mineral water and rainwater. You will also need some liquid soap, five jam jars with lids, and an eye dropper. The distilled water will have no salts in it, so it will not be hard. You can compare all your results with that of the distilled water. The distilled water is referred to as a control.

1 Fill half a jam jar with distilled water. Add 10 drops of liquid soap. Replace the lid and shake well. How much foam do you produce? Make a note of the amount of foam.

2 Repeat this test with all the other samples of water. Make sure you add the same amount of water to each jar. Which sample of water produced the most foam? How could you improve the design of this experiment? How could you modify this experiment to test shampoos?

What does boiling do to some types of hard water?

amount of polluting scum that was produced on the surface of rivers. The scum was produced when the soapy water was poured into hard water. Some rivers had a thick layer of soap suds on the surface of the water. However, the problem has now been largely solved with the introduction of soapless detergents, so that most washing liquids, powders and shampoos do not form a scum when used with hard water.

Some detergents react with chemicals in water to form an unattractive scum which floats on the surface.

Key words
Saturation the point at which no more of a substance will dissolve in a solvent.
Solute a substance that will dissolve in a solvent.
Solvent a substance such as water in which another substance will dissolve.

Water for transport and support

All organisms require a supply of water to survive. The water has many different functions, but two of the most common are to transport substances around the organism and actually to support the organism, either internally or externally. Today, large amounts of water are transported across huge distances in order to deliver it to people's homes. The water is carried from rivers, lakes and other storage areas to cities.

Water for transport

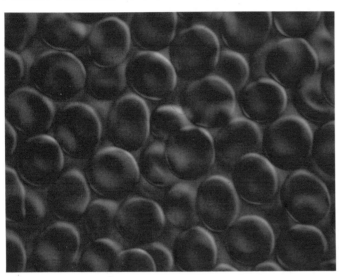

There are more than five billion red blood cells in every litre of blood. Their job is to carry oxygen to the cells. They are transported in fluid called plasma made up mainly of water.

Water makes up almost half of the volume of human blood. A person has around five litres of blood in their body, which is made up of two main parts, plasma and cells. The plasma is a sticky, straw-coloured liquid made up mostly of water. There are many substances dissolved in the water. Food materials, such as glucose, and amino acids are absorbed from the intestine and carried by the blood around the body to the individual cells. The blood also picks up waste material, such as urea. This diffuses from the cells and dissolves in the water of the plasma. The urea is carried by the blood to the kidneys (see page 41) where it is removed. Another waste product, carbon dioxide, is carried by the blood from the cells to the lungs. Special chemical messengers, called hormones, are also carried in the blood. Hormones have very specific roles in the body. For example, the hormone adrenaline prepares the body for either fight or flight. If you are frightened, it is released from a tiny gland near the kidney and carried to the organs of the body by the blood. It causes your heart to beat more quickly and makes you breathe more rapidly.

There are three types of cell suspended within the plasma: red blood cells, white blood cells and platelets. The red blood cells are responsible for transporting oxygen. They pick up oxygen in the lungs and carry it to every cell in the body. The white blood cells have an important role to play in the body's immune system. They destroy bacteria and other disease-causing organisms that gain entry to our bodies. The third type of cell, the platelets, are tiny fragments of cells. Their job is to help the blood to clot when a blood vessel is damaged.

Plants also rely on water for their internal transport system. They have two main tissues which are responsible for the movement of substances around the plant. One is a tissue called xylem. This is responsible for moving water and dissolved

! *Blood may look red but the liquid part of blood, the plasma, is colourless. The colour comes from a red pigment called haemoglobin.*

 What type of food material is found in potato tubers?

Celery sucks up water through xylem (the xylem vessels are dyed red in the lower stick of celery), just like sucking on a straw.

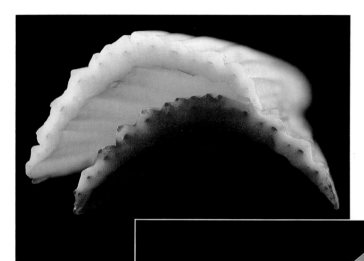

minerals from the roots to the parts of the plant above ground. The water flows up the tiny tubes called xylem vessels, which are rather like a bundle of drinking straws. When you drink using a straw, water is drawn up the straw because you suck at the top. Plants draw up water from the ground in a similar manner. As water evaporates from the surfaces of the leaves, more water is drawn upwards from the root and up the stem to replace it. This creates a continual flow of water from the roots to the leaves. The evaporation of water from the leaves is called transpiration.

Leaves have tiny pores, called stomata. Most of these are found on the under surface of the leaf. The stomata are designed to allow gases to enter and leave the plant for photosynthesis (the process of making food from carbon dioxide and water using light energy) and respiration (the process in which glucose and other food materials are broken down to release energy). When the stomata are open, water vapour can escape as well. Water loss is less at night because the stomata are closed. Many leaves have a shiny, wax-like, waterproof covering on the upper surface of their leaves, known as a cuticle. This covering helps to reduces water loss because plants with a waxy cuticle can only lose water through the stomata on the lower surfaces of each leaf.

The second plant transport system is called the phloem. This tissue is responsible for moving food materials like sucrose from the leaves to wherever it is needed. This may be in the new shoots or roots for growth, or in storage areas, such as carrot roots and potato tubers where the food is kept for later use.

What type of conditions would cause the greatest amount of transpiration from a leaf?

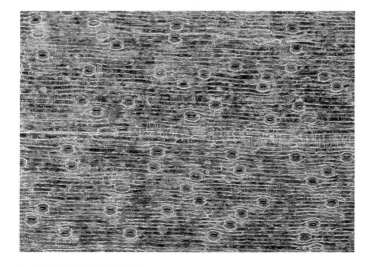

The underside of this leaf of a hyacinth plant has many pores called stomata. When the stomata are open water vapour can escape into the air.

EXPERIMENT

Investigating transpiration

This experiment investigates the rate at which a pot plant loses water. All you will need for this experiment is a small potted plant such as a busy lizzie or geranium, two plastic bags, two elastic bands and some scales.

1 Water the plant and allow any excess water to drain away.

2 Place a small plastic bag around the pot and secure the bag in position using an elastic band around the stem (see photograph). This will prevent water from evaporating from the soil and affecting the results.

3 Weigh your plant and then place it on a sunny window ledge. Leave the plant there for several hours and then reweigh it. Make a note of the new weight, and work out the loss in mass by subtracting the new weight from the original weight.

4 You will need to replace the water before you start the next stage. Take a container and weigh out the same amount of water as was lost by the plant. Undo the elastic band and add the water to the soil. Replace the elastic band. Place the plant in a cupboard so that it is in the dark. Leave it for the same amount of time as before and then reweigh the plant. Make a note of the new weight and again calculate the weight loss. Did the plant lose more weight in the dark or on the window ledge?

5 Now repeat the experiment, but this time place a second plastic bag around the whole plant. Keep the first bag around the pot. What effect did the presence of the second plastic bag have on the results?

How could you prove that the loss in weight is due to the evaporation of water? Would the plant lose more or less water if it was placed in a windy, sunny place (see page 30)?

Artificial water transport systems

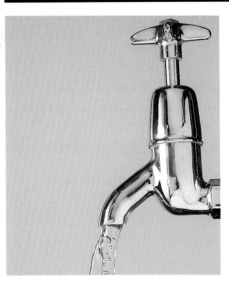

Artificially transported water often ends up coming out of a tap.

Most people in the western world expect to see water come out of a tap when they turn it on. But how does the water get there? Most modern cities are built with a network of underground pipes bringing in water, gas and oil and taking away sewage and other waste water.

Water can be carried over great distances from places where there is plenty of water to areas where there is less. A channel that is designed to move water across a valley is called an aqueduct. The first aqueducts were built by the ancient Greeks more than two and a half thousand years ago. New ways of transporting water are still being developed. The California State Water Project has involved transporting water from Lake Oroville, in the north of the state, over approximately 177 km across the Techachapi mountains to the urban areas of southern California.

Water can be transported over great distances naturally in water-bearing rocks. Aquifers are rocks which retain a lot of water

within them. They form underground stores of water. Aquifers can carry water underground over thousands of kilometres, although the water flows through the rocks at a very, very slow rate. There are a number of large aquifers in North Africa, for example in Egypt. In this part of the world it may be as long as 40,000 years between the time the rain fell and the time it reaches the surface again! There is, in fact, a considerable store of water beneath the Sahara.

When an aquifer comes to the surface the water can escape, forming a spring. Many settlements have grown up around natural springs which provide a supply of fresh drinking water. In the desert there are watering holes

Huge water pipes are one way of carrying water over large distances, either for use in cities or for generating electricity.

A geyser is a natural spring that discharges an explosive column of steam and hot water. Old Faithful in Yellowstone National Park, USA discharges water every 33 to 96 minutes.

The Pont du Gard is a well known Roman aqueduct near Nîmes, France. During Roman times it delivered 20,000 m³ of water to Nîmes every day.

Canal systems such as this one in California carry water over great distances.

Many plants and animals make use of water from a natural spring, like the one on the right. People have been able to tap into the water held in aquifers by digging down into the ground until they find water. Wells are often deep holes that require pumps to bring the water to the surface.

called oases. An oasis is a place in a desert where the ground surface meets an aquifer, for example in a valley.

Many cities rely on water from underground aquifers. The water is extracted by drilling through the overlying rock to form an artificial spring, or well. Wells can also tap the water table. The water table is the level to which water will filter down through the ground and then collect.

Water for support

The world's largest animals, whales, are only able to grow to such a large size because they are supported by water.

Water is almost impossible to compress (press into a smaller volume). This feature of water allows it to be used as a form of support by many smaller plants. Although such plants do not have a skeleton, they do have cells with strengthened walls. The cell is filled with a gel-like substance called cytoplasm. The cytoplasm contains a lot of water. Plant cells also contain a large vacuole (a fluid-filled structure bound by a membrane). The vacuole holds a lot of water. If the plant cell takes up more water, the cytoplasm and the vacuole fill with water and become swollen. This causes the contents of the cell to push against the cell wall. These cells are described as being turgid and turgid cells make the plant stiffer and better able to stand up to forces such as wind.

The importance of water is clearly demonstrated by a plant that has not had enough water because it soon starts to wilt. As the cells lose water, so the plant loses its support and the leaves begin to collapse. If the plant is quickly given some water, the cells can recover. However, if a plant is allowed to remain without water for too long, the cells will be permanently damaged and the plant will die.

This giant kelp is supported by the water. When it is washed up on a shore it collapses into a pile.

Animals and plants that live in water rely on water for support. Animals such as jelly fish do not have a skeleton but rely on water to support their body organs. There are also large plants living in water. Large land-living plants such as the trees have to produce wood to support their trunks. Some of the largest seaweeds are many hundreds of metres in length and they gain all the support they need from the water. When they are washed up on to the shore they collapse as they have lost their means of support.

Many animals rely on water for internal support. Worms, such as the marine fireworm, have a central cavity that contains water. The worm's muscles push on the fluid but the fluid cannot compress, so it is forced towards one end of the worm. By controlling the pressure on the fluid and where it is applied, the muscles can cause the worm's body to change shape. By using one set of muscles, the front end of its body extends forwards, while another set causes the back part of its body to contract and move towards the front end. By repeating this process, the worm can move its whole body forwards.

People also make use of the fact that water is impossible to compress. Many machines contain a hydraulic system, that is, a system of tubes filled with a liquid — often water. Since the liquid cannot be compressed, a force applied to the liquid is transmitted through the liquid and transferred to something else. Hydraulic car brakes work because the liquid inside the braking system cannot be compressed.

The fireworm (above) and the hydraulic arm of the digger (right) both make use of hydraulic pressure.

Key words
Aquifer a rock capable of bearing water.
Blood a thick, sticky liquid flowing in blood vessels, consisting of cells suspended in plasma.
Transpiration the evaporation of water from a plant, mostly from the leaves.

Fresh and salt water

At the dawn of the earth's history, more than 4600 million years ago, there were no oceans and there was no atmosphere. Heat from within the planet caused some substances to evaporate and build up a layer of gas around the planet, thus creating the atmosphere. One of these gases was water vapour, the gaseous form of water. As the temperature of the atmosphere decreased there was more water present than the atmosphere could hold, so much of the vapour condensed into a liquid, falling as rain to form the oceans. This water was not pure as it contained many elements such as chlorine, bromine, iodine, and nitrogen. Since the oceans were first formed, other substances, such as minerals from eroded rocks, have been washed into them by rivers. It is these minerals, in particular sodium chloride, that make the oceans salty.

Although we specifically describe the water of the seas and oceans as salt water, almost all water contains dissolved salts, as well as dissolved gases and organic matter. (More recently water also contains pollutants.) The main difference between fresh water and salt water is the quantity of salts present. One litre of sea water contains approximately 35 g of salt, although this does vary around the world. The most common salt is sodium chloride or common salt, but there are also salts of magnesium and calcium (see page 16). In fact, salt water contains small amounts of virtually all elements found on the planet earth.

Brackish water is salt water mixed with fresh water. It often occurs at the mouths of rivers where they meet the sea, and as far upstream as they are affected by the tides. Fresh water is also affected by the rock and soil over which the water runs. The minute amounts of salt present determine whether the water is hard or soft (see page 16).

The water level in Lake Mono, California, is falling, leaving behind encrustations of a salty substance called calcite.

The Great Salt Lake in Utah, USA, and the Dead Sea in Israel have so much salt in them that it crystallises on the shoreline.

Diffusion and osmosis

If you carefully release a small amount of coloured ink into some still water, the ink slowly spreads through the water until the water is evenly coloured. The molecules of the ink have become evenly distributed throughout the water. The movement of the molecules from a place where they are in high concentration to one where they are in low concentration is called diffusion.

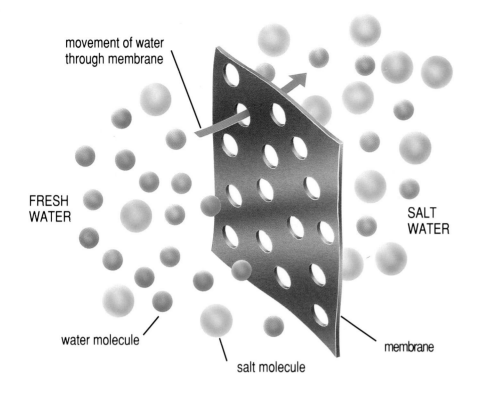

movement of water
through membrane

FRESH
WATER

SALT
WATER

water molecule

salt molecule

membrane

When fresh water and salt water are separated by a partially permeable membrane, water on the fresh water side will move across to the salt water side.

All cells are surrounded by a cell membrane which has tiny holes in it. These holes allow some smaller molecules to pass in and out of the cell, while preventing the passage of larger ones. This means that the cell can control what substances enter or leave the cell. The membrane is described as being partially permeable. The water molecule is very small so it can cross the cell membrane. So, if there is a lot of water around the cell and less water inside the cell, water will move through the membrane into the cell. This movement is a form of diffusion called osmosis. As the cell gains water through osmosis, it will swell up. In certain situations cells can also lose water. For example, if they are surrounded by a concentrated salt solution, osmosis will cause the water to leave the cell, which will shrink and possibly die.

EXPERIMENT

Osmosis in potatoes

In this experiment you will investigate the effect of osmosis in potatoes. You will need some potatoes, a watch, a teaspoon, a knife and a small amount of sugar and salt.
1 Carefully cut a potato in half using the knife. Then cut out a small depression in the surface of each half of the potato (see photograph). Also slice off a small amount to flatten the bottom of each potato half so that,

placed with the depression uppermost, they will not fall over.
2 Put half a level teaspoon of salt into the depression in one potato half.
3 Add one level teaspoon of salt to the depression in the other half of the potato. Leave both potato halves for one hour.
4 Look again at the holes after one hour. Can you see any fluid?
5 Repeat this experiment with another potato, using sugar rather than salt.
6 Repeat the experiment, but this time add one teaspoon of water instead of salt or sugar.
You should find that the presence of salt or sugar in the depression causes water to be drawn by osmosis from the potato. The water is moving by osmosis, from where there is lots of water (the potato cells) to where there is less (the salt or sugar). When you placed water in the depression, the volume of water there after one hour should have decreased. Why?

Living in fresh water

What would happen to fresh water organisms if they could not get rid of the excess water?

Animals that live in fresh water are faced with a problem. They are surrounded by a lot of water. The cells of their body are full of salts, so there is less water inside their cells compared to outside. Since osmosis can occur across their cell membranes, water will always try to move into their body from the outside. These animals have to continually get rid of the excess water. The amoeba is one of the simplest possible living organisms. It is unicellular (only has one cell). Since it lives in fresh water, water is always passing across its cell membrane into the cell. The amoeba has to pump out this excess water, almost as though it was baling out a leaky boat! It has a special structure called a contractile vacuole which repeatedly fills with water, moves to the surface of the cell and pumps water out.

Many larger animals have developed impermeable surfaces that reduce the amount of water entering their body. For example, fish are covered with scales which are impermeable to water. Even the human skin is relatively waterproof. This means that, if you sit in the bath for a long time, thankfully your body will not swell up with water!

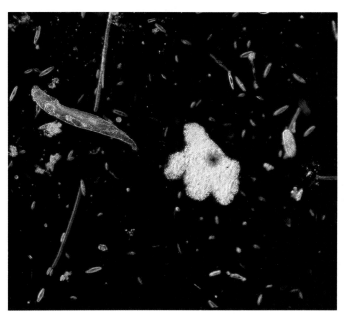

The amoeba relies on its contractile vacuole to pump the excess water out of its body. You can see the dark round vacuole in the middle of the white amoeba.

Living in salt water

Animals that live in salt water have cells which contain a weaker salt solution than the surrounding sea. Due to the natural process of osmosis, water would want to leave their cells. If too much water left their bodies, they would dehydrate and eventually die. They also face another problem connected with the salt water. If they drink the sea water, they would consume a lot of salts which their bodies do not need and which could be damaging to them.

A turtle has a salt gland near its eye which removes excess salt from its body.

These salmon are returning to the river where they were born. Once there they will breed and complete their life cycle.

! *A salmon can smell the waters of its home river even when these are diluted to one part in several million.*

Many marine organisms survive in the sea by altering the salt concentration of the fluid in their cells so that it is exactly the same concentration as the surrounding water. This means that there will be no gain or loss of water. Some marine creatures remove unwanted salts from their bodies by pumping them out through a specially adapted gland.

The salmon is an unusual fish. Its young hatch from eggs laid in fresh water, but after only a few months they swim downstream and out to sea, where they mature. When the adult salmon is ready to spawn (to mate and lay eggs), it can always find its way back to the very river in which it was born. Salmon seem to have a remarkable ability to identify their native river by detecting the presence of minerals and other substances in its waters. They swim upstream to spawn, and so complete their life cycle. Many species of salmon die immediately after spawning, but others return to the sea and repeat the process for several years. To be able to live in fresh and salt water at the various different stages of their lives, salmon have evolved the remarkable ability to alter the whole chemistry of their bodies to cope with either environment.

Using salt water

Salt can be extracted from salt water by allowing the water to evaporate in the sun. The salt left behind can be collected.

People can drink fresh water, but not salt water. If we drink salt water we become very ill as our body cannot cope with the salts. In places where fresh water is in short supply, such as in desert areas near the equator, desalination plants provide an important source of fresh water. Desalination is a process in which the salt is removed from sea water. The fresh water can then be used for drinking or to irrigate crops. In the past, most desalination plants relied upon distillation to remove the salt. The salt water was placed in a vessel and heated so that it boiled. The water vapour was drawn off and then cooled. This caused the water vapour to condense, allowing pure water to be collected. Impurities in the water, such as salts, were left in the vessel. The water that was produced was even purer than normal fresh water. This method was quite expensive,

Why do scientists distill water before they use it in experiments?

because it required large amounts of energy to boil off the water but, in the 1970s a process called reverse osmosis was developed. In this process, an artificial membrane is used to remove the molecules of salt from the water.

Many arid (dry) parts of the world, for example the Middle East, Mediterranean and parts of the southern USA, do not receive enough water from rain to sustain agriculture. However, it is often possible to supplement the natural water supply by irrigation techniques. These involve taking water from where there is plenty and moving it along canals to where it is needed. Alternatively, deep wells are sometimes dug to extract water from the water table many metres below the surface (see page 22).

Only one third of the water sprayed on to this field in California will be taken up by the plants.

Nearly three quarters of all the fresh water used by people is for irrigation. However, irrigation is quite an inefficient use of water, since only one third of the water is actually taken up by the crops. The rest either runs off the land, moves down to the water table or simply evaporates in the sun. Many farmers in the USA and Australia are discovering that too much irrigation can cause unexpected problems. If too much water is put on the land, the excess water quickly evaporates from the surface in the hot climate. As the water evaporates from the surface it draws up more water from below. This water carries salts to the top layers of soil. Deposits of salt build up and eventually become visible as whitish streaks on the surface of the soil. This process is called salination. After a few years, the soil becomes so degraded (spoiled) that it can no longer be used for farming.

Irrigation schemes are found throughout the world. There are approximately 270 million hectares of irrigated land in use, an area the size of India. Today, almost one third of this area is affected by salination. Even in the USA, where irrigation is more carefully controlled, approximately 20 per cent of the irrigated land is now affected to some degree. Salination is being studied particularly carefully in Australia, where thousands of hectares of land have already been ruined by salination.

Increasing amounts of salt in the soil has caused these trees in Australia to die.

It is estimated that 25-30 million hectares of irrigated land has been so badly damaged by salination that it can never again be used for farming.

The sea lavender can survive on the edge of salt marshes.

Rice is grown in fresh water paddies. In the future new varieties of rice may be grown in salt water.

Many land plants would be killed by concentrations of salt just one tenth of that in salt water. However, plants that live in salt marshes and salt deserts can tolerate quite high salt concentrations. A salt marsh is a complex maze of muddy channels. It is usually found in river estuaries near the coast. Plants that grow in this salty habitat may be surrounded by water, but most of it is salt water and so is useless to them. They may have to survive for many weeks before rain or floodwaters bring fresh water. This means that such plants have to be able to conserve water, rather like the cacti of desert habitats (see page 34). Many salt marsh plants have small, fleshy leaves with a thick waxy cuticle to reduce water loss by evaporation. Some have a membrane covering their roots which prevents the salts from gaining entry. Other plants get rid of the salt through glands on their leaves.

Rice is the only major cereal crop that actually grows in fresh water. Young rice plants are transplanted into water-filled fields, called paddies. Raised mud banks retain the water during the growing period. Researchers have been trying to improve rice's tolerance to salt so that it might be grown on land contaminated by salt water after a flood, or on natural salt marshes along coasts. This may become particularly important if global warming continues. One effect of global warming could be rising sea levels that would flood low-lying land with sea water. It would be important to keep this land productive for growing food.

Key words
Desalination the removal of salt from sea water.
Diffusion the movement of molecules from an area where they are in high concentration to one where they are in lower concentration.
Irrigation the watering of crops by artificial means.
Osmosis the movement of water molecules from a place where they are in high concentration to one where they are in lower concentration through a partially permeable membrane.

Water for cooling

It takes a lot of heat energy to change water from its liquid state into water vapour. This physical fact is commonly made use of in cooling systems. Engines, for example, generate a lot of excess heat energy. In order to prevent an engine from overheating, this heat must be removed by cooling. Water is one of the most common forms of coolant, because it is plentiful and uses up lots of heat energy in the evaporative process.

Natural cooling

There are approximately five million sweat glands in an adult human body. On a hot day, a human being can lose more than two litres of sweat.

An athlete will sweat to cool down naturally. But sitting in a shower of cold water also helps!

The kangaroo cools itself by licking the skin of its forearm.

The human body can be thought of as a form of engine. The food we eat is digested and absorbed into our body. Once it reaches a cell, the chemical energy from the food can be released and used for the processes that take place in the cell. This process is called respiration. However, quite a lot of heat energy is also released. Most of the time, this helps to keep our bodies at our normal temperature of 37°C. But, if we do strenuous physical exercise, or we are in a hot environment, excess heat energy has to be dissipated (got rid of) or the body will overheat. The body uses water to help it keep cool by sweating. The skin contains millions of tiny sweat glands which produce water with a little urea (see page 41) and some salts dissolved in it. The liquid travels up a duct from the sweat glands, which actually lie quite deep in the skin, to the surface of the skin. As the sweat lies on the surface, the water takes heat energy from the skin and evaporates, thereby cooling the skin.

Sometimes it is difficult for the sweat to evaporate. For example, in a hot and humid climate, sweat often lies on the surface of the skin and does not evaporate. This is because the air already contains so much water vapour that no more water can evaporate. Instead, it stays on the skin and makes the person feel sticky and uncomfortable. In a hot, dry climate, however, the air contains little water vapour, so any sweat quickly evaporates, making us feel cooler. A similar effect is felt when it is windy. Wind carries the water vapour away from the skin more rapidly, and replaces it with dry air capable of absorbing more moisture.

Very few mammals are able to sweat. Most mammals have evolved other ways of keeping cool in hot weather. Kangaroos have a network of tiny capillaries very near the surface of the skin along their forearm. They lick the fur above this area of skin, and the blood is cooled as the saliva evaporates and heat is drawn from the capillaries below. Dogs hang their tongues out and pant. These quick, shallow breaths bring cool dry air into the body and allows lots of water to evaporate from the tongue and the rest of the mouth, so cooling the blood. Cats lick themselves in order to spread a thin layer of saliva over their fur. As the saliva evaporates, it cools the body.

Camels live in dry desert areas where water is in short supply. They cannot afford the luxury of being able to lose water by sweating. Nevertheless, camels still need some means of keeping cool. While most mammals keep their body temperature within a very narrow range day and night (in humans within a fraction of a degree above or below 37°C), camels allow their body temperature to fluctuate. During the heat of the day, they allow their body temperature to rise. By the end of the day their body temperature may be as much as 6°C higher than it was in the morning. At night, deserts are quite cold places as there are few clouds to retain the heat. So as night-time temperatures drop, the body temperature of the camel falls back to its lowest level. It has been estimated that by allowing the body temperature to rise and fall naturally in this way the camel saves approximately six litres of water which would otherwise have been lost as sweat. A further adaptation of the camel, designed to save even more water, is the production of very concentrated urine.

Camels conserve their body water by never sweating.

Why do you feel less comfortable on a still, humid day than on a hot and windy day?

Cooling engines and power stations

Water is used as a coolant in car engines. Cool water is pumped around the cylinders of the engine where the fuel is burnt, removing excess heat. From there it is passed through the radiator where it loses its heat energy to the air. A car radiator is said to be a form of heat exchanger. The hot water in the tubes of the radiator comes into contact with cooler air from outside and the heat energy is transferred to the air. The water in the radiator is therefore cooler than when it entered the radiator. When the car is moving, air is forced over the radiator. However, engines could overheat while the car is stationary or moving very slowly. Therefore a fan is often provided to force air over the radiator if the car is stationary. The cool water from the radiator then passes back around the cylinders. Some of the hot water passes through a smaller heat exchanger from which hot air can be used to heat the passenger compartment of the car in winter. In cold weather, an antifreeze is added to the water in the coolant system to stop it from freezing and cracking the pipes of the radiator (see page 11).

The engine of this Norton motor bike is kept cool by cylinders filled with water running over the parts of the engine that get hot.

Water is frequently used as a coolant in power stations. Most power stations are built beside a river or by the sea from which an adequate supply of water can be pumped easily and cheaply. A coal-fired power station burns coal inside a furnace. The heat is used to turn water into high pressure steam. This steam turns huge fans, called steam turbines, that are coupled to electromagnets called rotors. The rotors revolve inside a stationary coil of copper wire and generate electricity. The whole process involves two transformations of energy: the heat energy in the steam is transformed into kinetic (movement) energy in the rotating turbines and rotors. This kinetic energy is then converted into electrical energy.

Although the steam is cooler when it leaves the turbine, it is not cool enough to condense back into water. To reduce its temperature and make it return to its liquid state, the steam passes through enormous cooling towers where it comes into contact with tubes containing cold water from the river or sea. The steam thus

---

EXPERIMENT

Evaporative cooling

In this experiment you will investigate the effect of evaporation on the rate at which water cools. You will need four small jam jars with lids, a screw driver, a thermometer, some cotton wool, two small containers and some warm and cold tap water.

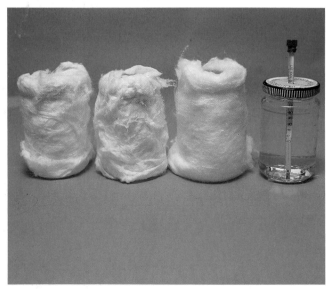

1 Make a hole with the screw driver in each of the lids, large enough to allow the thermometer to be pushed through.
2 Fill all four jam jars with tap water and replace the lids. Make a note of the temperature of the water.
3 Soak some cotton wool in warm tap water for a couple of minutes. At the same time soak some cotton wool in cold tap water.
4 The next stage must be carried out quickly as the experiment will start as soon as you place the cotton wool in position. Surround one jar with dry cotton wool. Surround the second jar with cotton wool that has been soaked in warm water and surround the third jar with cotton wool soaked in cold water. Do not place any cotton wool around the fourth jar. This jar will be the control. You should compare all your results to those of the control.
5 Take temperature readings every few minutes for approximately 20 minutes. Which jar cooled the most rapidly? How could you improve the design of this experiment?

cools further and condenses. It is then returned to the furnace. The sea or river water in the tubes, now several degrees warmer, will be pumped back to where it came. In some places, the warm water leaving the power station is sufficient to keep the nearby water ice-free all winter. For example, in northern Canada many birds are attracted to the ice-free lakes beside power stations because it allows them to feed all through the winter.

In some power stations, where there are factories and buildings nearby, the warm waste water from the power station is not released into the river, but is used as a cheap source of heat to warm the buildings during the winter. This makes the power station more efficient.

The warm water pumped out of this nuclear power station in California has been used to create a recreational lake.

Water for heat storage

Why does a coal-fired power station need a supply of water?

A large body of water will absorb heat energy quite slowly. It will also release this heat energy slowly, so it takes a long time to cool down (see page 9). The high heat capacity of water has many uses. Since the earliest times, water has been used to keep homes cool in summer. For example, people would take frozen blocks of ice from lakes and pack them away in sawdust to cool food during the summer months. Now that ways of producing energy are becoming even more expensive, many small scale heating and cooling projects are being developed all around the world.

Scientists are developing ways of storing the heat energy of summer sunlight and using it for winter heating. In the USA, the University of Massachusetts at Amhurst is building a central solar heating plant designed to capture the heat energy of the sun and to store it in the ground for use later in the year. During the summer months, south-facing solar collectors will absorb the heat energy and transfer it, via a heat exchanger, to a mixture of water and alcohol (the alcohol acts as an antifreeze, see page 11). The warm water and alcohol mix is pumped through thousands of plastic pipes sunk deep in the ground, releasing the heat energy which warms the clay soil. By midsummer the clay will reach temperatures of 50°C or more. Some heat energy will be diverted to a spare water tank to provide hot water at night when the solar collectors are not working. During the cold winter months, cold water flowing through the buried pipes will absorb the stored heat energy from the clay. The warm water will be circulated around pipes in the university buildings, keeping them warm.

Key words
Evaporation a change in state from liquid to gas.
Sweating the evaporation of sweat from the surface of the skin.

Water storage and conservation

Water is a rare resource in many parts of the world. Deserts, by definition, are places where there is very little water for almost all of the year. When it eventually does rain, it usually comes all at once in heavy downpours, often causing floods. In many other climatic areas of the world there are rainy seasons and dry seasons. In these places, water has to be used carefully and stored for use in the dry seasons.

Desert adaptations

The candelabra cactus grows in the deserts of South America.

Desert plants have to be able to survive for months, and sometimes even years, without a supply of water. Plants that show special adaptations to conserve or store water are called xerophytes. Cacti and succulents are the most common examples. They have small leaves, so less water evaporates from their surfaces. In extreme cases the leaf has been reduced to a spine. The leaves are usually covered with a thick, waxy layer or cuticle to reduce water loss (see page 19). Many species of cacti are covered in a layer of white hairs. The white colour reflects heat away from the plant, while the hairs trap a thin layer of air around the plant, making it more difficult for water to evaporate. Some plants, such as the giant fig, have evolved incredibly deep roots able to reach down to the water table many metres below ground. Others have a shallow but wide root system. This is designed so that, when it rains, the roots can absorb water from as large an area as possible. Many cacti are shaped like a barrel so that liquid can be stored within the stems. Often this liquid is quite acid to the taste, but one or two cacti contain sweet, fresh water that is safe to drink.

Cacti and succulents are not the only plants that live in deserts. Annual plants (plants that live for just one year) live there too, sometimes surviving only for a few weeks, just long enough to produce seeds before dying. The landscape in a desert is transformed after rain, for the annual plants have to complete their life cycles very quickly. As soon as the rain falls, the seeds in the ground germinate and within a

The thorny devil lives in the deserts of Central Australia. It stores water in the fatty lumps on its body.

The welwitschia is an unusually large desert plant that can live with little water for hundreds of years.

The dung of a camel is so dry that it can be used as a fuel almost as soon as it hits the ground.

Can you think of five ways in which a cactus is adapted to living in a desert?

few weeks they flower and produce seeds. These seeds may have to stay dormant in the ground for several years until it rains again when they, in turn, can germinate.

Animals also need water to survive, so those that live in deserts have to be specially adapted to conserve water. The camel saves water by not sweating and by allowing its body temperature to rise (see page 31). The kangaroo rat never needs to drink water since it gains all the water it needs from its food. Water is released as food substances are respired, or broken down, within each cell. This water, called metabolic water, is just sufficient to enable the kangaroo rat to survive. Desert predators, such as the fennec fox and the jackal, obtain the water they require from the bodies of the animals they kill and eat.

The Namib Desert in southwest Africa is different from other deserts. Although it rarely rains, the desert is close to the coast and is sometimes covered by fog. On several nights each year, the fog moves over the desert and, as it does so, tiny droplets of water condense in the cool air and fall to the ground. Many animals and plants have developed behaviour patterns to make use of this water supply. Darkling beetles, which have very long legs, clamber to the top of sand dunes and align themselves to face the coast. The beetle will raise its abdomen and, as the fog moves past, droplets of water condense on to it and roll down into its open mouth. The Namib Desert is also home to an unusual plant called welwitschia. It does not resemble a conventional desert plant, because rather than having small leaves, welwitschia has huge leaves, each being several metres long. Running beneath the upper surface of the leaf are absorbent fibres. These fibres are specially adapted to absorb any moisture that condenses on the surface.

EXPERIMENT

Water from the ground

In this experiment you will obtain a supply of fresh water from the ground. This experiment demonstrates a method that can be used to get water in a desert. You will need a spade, a small container in which to collect the water, a piece of plastic sheeting, a ruler and some large stones. You should carry out this experiment on a sunny day.

1 Dig a hole in the ground that is approximately four times the length of the

container. The hole should have steeply sloping sides. Place the container at the bottom of the hole.

2 Stretch the piece of plastic across the hole and secure it in place with stones around the edge. Place a large stone in the middle of the plastic, immediately above the container, and allow the plastic to drop down into the hole slightly.

3 Leave the container for an hour and then examine it. Measure how much water you collect. Look again after another hour and continue through the day.

The amount of water collected increases as the day progresses. The heat of the sun has caused water vapour to condense on the inside of the plastic sheeting. The water then runs towards the lowest point, from which it drips into the container.

This is a very simple experiment that could be improved. How could you design an experiment to investigate the effect of the depth of hole or the colour of the plastic on the amount of water collected?

Storing water

A large reservoir has formed behind the Shasta Dam in California, USA. It not only stores water, but also produces electricity when water leaves the reservoir.

In order to provide a year-round supply of water, engineers have developed ways of collecting and storing water for future use. A common way of storing water is to build a reservoir. This is a large lake, usually formed by damming a river, which prevents the water from flowing down the valley. After rain, the level of water stored in the reservoir increases until it nearly reaches the top of the dam. The water can be used at any time, and is often pumped into a canal or pipeline which takes it to the local cities or to the farmlands where the water is to be used. The River Colorado in the USA has been dammed in several places. The water is used to irrigate land that would otherwise be too dry for agriculture (see page 28) and to provide drinking water for cities like Phoenix. The Glen Canyon and Hoover dams also have turbines positioned at the bottom of the dam which are turned by falling water.

Can you think of some of the disadvantages of building reservoirs?

Many thousands of hectares of rainforest were flooded when the Kenyir Dam was built in Malaya. Dead trees can still be seen at the edge of the water.

The reservoir behind Owens Falls Dam in Uganda stores an amazing 204 billion m³ of water.

Key words
Adaptation a change in response to the environment.
Reservoir a large store of water, often formed by damming a river.
Xerophyte a plant adapted to surviving in dry conditions.

The kinetic energy of the falling water is transformed into electrical energy, which is used by nearby towns, including Las Vegas. Electricity generated in this way is known as hydroelectric power. The dam does not have to be large to generate hydroelectricity. Even quite small dams in remote mountain streams can generate enough power for limited local use.

However, there are problems associated with building dams. Because the river is prevented from flooding, silt will no longer be washed downstream and deposited on farmland, and the benefit of this natural fertilisation process is lost. Since less water flows along the river, the ecology of the river downstream from the dam is affected. Upstream of the dam, the reservoir will flood many hectares, thereby destroying a large part of the natural habitat in the river valley. Some of the dams that have been built in tropical countries have flooded huge tracts of unspoilt rainforest.

The Aswan High Dam was built on the River Nile during the 1960s. It was designed to keep the flow of water in the River Nile at a constant level all year and so prevent flooding. Unfortunately the annual floods used to bring down a lot of silt which was deposited on the agricultural land either side of the Lower Nile in Egypt. This made the soil very fertile. Now farmers have to fertilise their land because the river never floods. Instead the silt is collecting in the lake behind the dam. Another problem is the decreasing amount of water coming down the Nile from the highlands to the south of Egypt. The level in the lake has fallen by 20 metres, threatening the hydroelectric power generation.

In desert areas a new design of dam, called the underground dam, is proving very useful. Since the water is stored below ground the amount of water lost by evaporation is much reduced.

Cleaning water

Many ponds and rivers in the industrial world are now heavily polluted with industrial and domestic waste. This pond is polluted with phosphates.

A typical New York resident uses more than 300 litres of water every day while, on average, a Kenyan uses only 5 litres of water.

It is essential to have a supply of clean, fresh water for drinking. Water taken from underground wells or reservoirs or from rivers is never completely pure. It will contain many living organisms, including bacteria. Most of these bacteria are harmless, but some can cause serious diseases such as cholera, dysentery and typhoid. There will also be dissolved gases, such as oxygen and carbon dioxide, and minerals such as calcium and magnesium that have come from the rocks through which the water passes (see page 12). Solid particles of sand, silt and clay and grit will have been picked up by the water and held in suspension (mix of small particles and a liquid). Organic matter will be present, too, from the remains of twigs and leaves or even dead animals. The water may also contain dissolved chemicals such as nitrates, phosphates and sulphates. These are much more common nowadays, for they are used extensively to spray crops and fertilise farmland. They may also have been washed into the water as factory or human sewage waste. In severe cases, the water may be badly polluted by such industrial and human wastes.

Due to the wide range of possible contaminants, public water supplies have to be purified before the water is safe to drink. In most countries this is carried out at special water treatment plants. However, it should be appreciated that, for many people living in the developing world, a supply of clean water is very rare.

Water and sewage treatments

Every household in the developed world produces a lot of waste water from the toilets, the bath, dish washing water and more besides that goes down the drain into the sewers. This water has to be cleaned before it can be used again or returned to a river.

Sewage plants treat and clean our waste water. First, all the large pieces of rubbish in the water, such as paper and rags, must be screened out. The sewage then flows into a settling tank where the largest particles are separated out. The liquid waste then passes into a sedimentation tank, where the smaller pieces of waste sink to the bottom. The layer that forms at the bottom of the tank is called sludge. It contains many harmful bacteria and other substances and, perhaps unsurprisingly, does not smell very nice. The liquid from the sedimentation tank passes to a filter bed where it is sprinkled on to a bed of small stones (up to 2 m thick) and allowed slowly to filter down. There are lots of bacteria on the surface of the stones that digest any remaining organic matter in the liquid. In fact, there are a lot of other animals present too, feeding on the bacteria. These worms, beetles, springtails and flies help to keep the numbers of bacteria in check, because otherwise they would multiply uncontrollably and block up the filter bed.

It is estimated that more than 3,500,000 children world-wide die of dehydration caused by diarrhoea, contracted through drinking contaminated water.

Why is it important for water to be purified before being consumed?

Both the water treatment plant (right) and this swamp in Kenya (above) make use of the ability of bacteria and plants to clean water. Bacteria in the filter beds digest organic matter in sewage while the swamp plants take up impurities.

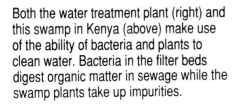

Some sewage farms use an aeration tank rather than a filter bed, although the basic purification principle is exactly the same. This is called the activated sludge method. Instead of passing the liquid over a filter bed, a stream of bubbles is blown through the

EXPERIMENT

A sand filter

In this experiment you will make a simple sand filter to clean dirty water. You will need an old plastic bottle, some coarse gravel, some fine gravel, some sand, a screwdriver and a pair of scissors.

1 Cut off the neck of the bottle and, using the screwdriver or similar pointed object, carefully make six small holes in the bottom of the bottle.

2 Place a layer of coarse gravel on the bottom, then a layer of fine gravel and finally a layer of sand. Make sure you leave enough space at the top to add the water.

3 Add some 'dirty' water to the top of the filter. This could be water from a pond or water that has been used for washing dishes. Keep a small amount of the dirty water back in order to compare the dirty sample with the filtered water.

4 Collect the filtered water as it drips from the bottom of the bottle. Compare this water with the dirty water. Does the water look clearer? N.B. DO NOT DRINK THE WATER. What effect do you think increasing the length of the filter would have on its cleaning powers?

Water from treatment plants in Florida is now sent to marshes planted specifically to filter out excess phosphates before water reaches the Everglades.

liquid, and bacteria feed on the organic matter in the water. The liquid is then passed into a second sedimentation tank where any remaining particles of organic matter settle out.

In both these systems, the bacteria digest and thereby neutralise any toxic or infectious substances. This use of bacteria is called microbial oxidation, and it is an essential part of the process of water cleansing. Water treated in this way is ready to be returned to the environment.

Plants, too, have been found to be capable of cleaning water containing either sewage or industrial waste materials. Plants such as reeds and rice can actually remove the impurities from the water as it circulates around their roots. Many of the impurities in sewage are nutrients such as nitrates and phosphates that plants actually need to grow.

A natural filter

Many of the chemical reactions that occur in living cells produce waste products. These waste products have to be removed, otherwise they would become toxic and harm the organism. The removal of these waste products is called excretion. One waste product the human body produces is urea, formed when the body breaks down protein. If we eat too much protein in our diet, our body cannot store the excess, so is forced to break it down instead. The liver breaks the protein down into urea which is taken to the kidneys for disposal.

The role of the kidney is to filter out all the unwanted substances. These substances include urea, excess salts and water and they are carried to the kidneys by the blood (see page 18). The waste substances form urine, which is passed on to the bladder for disposal. Mammals have two kidneys, near the back of the abdomen behind the intestine. Although a kidney looks quite solid, it contains millions of tiny tubes called nephrons. The arterial blood, containing the waste substances, passes into a kidney under high pressure, for it has come directly from the heart. Inside the kidney the artery divides into smaller and smaller blood vessels and eventually the blood enters a knot of tiny blood vessels. The blood pressure at this point is so high that the liquid part of the blood, the plasma, together with the dissolved waste products is squeezed out of the blood into a nephron. The walls of the blood vessels have tiny holes, so small that only molecules such as water,

? *Why do you often feel thirsty after eating a salty meal?*

! *The total length of blood vessels in both kidneys has been estimated at more than 160 km.*

The kidney (below) is the body's way of ridding itself of excess and harmful substances using water as the carrier. Patients with diseased kidneys have to be linked to a kidney dialysis machine for many hours a week (right).

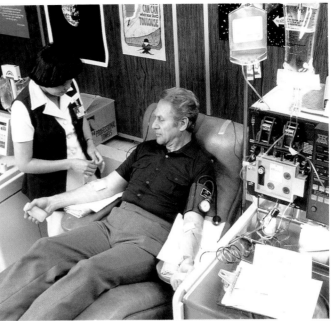

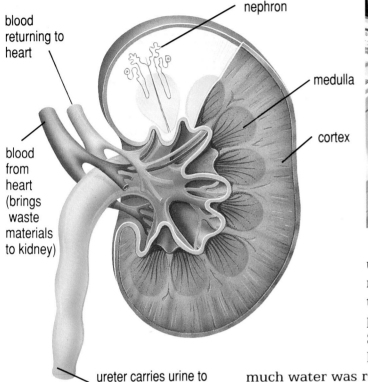

blood returning to heart

nephron

medulla

cortex

blood from heart (brings waste materials to kidney)

ureter carries urine to bladder

Why is it better for a person to have a kidney transplant rather than receive long-term treatment on a kidney machine?

Key words
Filtration the separation of certain sized particles from other larger particles.
Excretion the removal of toxic waste products from a living organism.
Osmoregulation the control of the amount of water contained within an organism.
Purification the cleansing of a substance, such as water, of impurities.

urea and glucose can pass through into the nephron. The wall is like a sieve. Blood cells and the larger molecules such as proteins cannot pass through the walls so they stay in the blood. Some of the water is returned to the blood because the body would soon dehydrate if too much water was removed. Eventually just urea, excess water and salts are left in the nephron. These substances form urine which travels to the bladder, where it is stored and later released.

The kidney is also responsible for controlling the amount of water retained by the body. Every day, we eat food and take in fluid. Despite this, our weight remains relatively constant. The body has to balance the amount of fluid taken in with the amount that is passed out in urine and sweat. If we drink a lot of fluid, then a lot of urine will be passed to get rid of the excess water. The process of controlling the amount of water is called osmoregulation. The kidneys can increase or decrease the amount of water that leaves the body in urine. On a hot day, you will sweat a lot and not produce much urine. The same happens if you eat a salty meal. The body has to dilute the salt, so little urine will be produced. However, on a cold day or if you drink a lot of fluid, you will produce much more urine.

People with kidney disease have problems filtering their blood. Waste products can build up in the body and, if something is not done, the person could die. Most people with kidney disease have to spend periods connected to a kidney machine, which functions as an artificial kidney. However, it is a slow process, and the patient often has to spend up to 10 hours a day, three times a week, connected to the machine. The patient can help a little by monitoring his or her diet carefully. For example, if he or she does do not eat too much protein, their body will not have to excrete too much urea or salt.

The future

Fossil fuels, such as coal, oil and gas, are used to generate much of our electricity and to power our vehicles. As supplies of these valuable power sources dwindle, it seems sensible for scientists to look for energy from one of the most common resources available to us – water.

Wave power is a potential alternative energy source. There have been several designs of wave generator, some built on coastlines and others floating on the surface of the water. The coastal ones rely on waves being funnelled into a narrow gully, which leads up to a turbine. Water rushing up the gully compresses the air in front of it. The resulting jet of air turns the turbine blades to generate electricity. The alternative, open water system involves the use of a floating device which rides up and down on the waves. Some of these also rely on the water pushing on air which then turns an internal turbine. The CLAM system, designed in the UK, floats on the surface of the water, but is also anchored in place to the sea bed. Wave movement forces air into bags located along the side of the machine. The air pressure increases and, when it has built up sufficiently, it moves a turbine within the machine, generating electricity. The electricity is carried back to land via an underwater cable.

The CLAM generator floats on the surface of the water. Electricity is produced as the wave movement forces air into a generator.

The latest wave power design looks rather like a flying saucer floating on the surface of the sea. Underneath the float is a spring loaded pump which is attached to the sea bed. As the crest of the wave passes, the float is raised and the spring is stretched. As the trough of the wave passes the spring relaxes, and as it does so it pumps water into a turbine to generate electricity. This device may not be the most efficient at transforming energy, but it is cheap to make and simple to install and maintain. The floating wave generator could be used to provide power for coastal desalination plants as well as for communities in remote locations.

Water supply is one of the most important factors controlling the colonisation of desert areas. Scientists have recently rediscovered an old method of obtaining water using rocks. In this remarkable method, stones are piled into a pyramid shape, forming a structure called an aerial well. It works best in areas

A modern shopping mall has been set up in the middle of the Arizona desert in North America. It is able to survive because a vital supply of water is transported through the desert.

Mosses such as sphagnum have genes which enable them to survive dehydration.

which experience a wide fluctuation in temperature with hot days and cold nights. In the daytime the stones warm up slowly, but at night when the temperature drops they lose much of the heat and become cooler than the surrounding air. The stones in the middle remain cool even on the hottest days. Even dry air contains a small amount of water vapour, so at night when warm air passes over the cooler stones the vapour in the air condenses. This water can then be collected. Using these devices, enough moisture could be captured from the dry air to supply water to a small community. The ancient Greek city of Feodosiya, now in the Ukraine, had a water supply system consisting of 13 aerial wells, each nearly 14 metres tall. Scientists estimate that the system could have produced as much as 20,000 litres of water a day.

New varieties of grass may help to reduce the amount of water that is needed to keep lawns green in arid regions. In cities such as Phoenix, which is located in a desert, a huge amount of water is used to maintain lawns. The new varieties of grass come from crested wheatgrass, a species native to Iran and Turkey. These grasses need only one third of the amount of water required by most lawn grasses. They also grow more slowly, so they do not need to be cut so often.

Biologists are also studying mosses, which can survive extreme dehydration. Some mosses can survive even though 90 per cent of their cells are damaged by dehydration. They recover in just a few minutes once resupplied with water. Biologists are hoping to be able to identify the gene that repairs the cell damage. They could then transfer the gene to other plants, for example grasses, in order to make them more resistant to drought.

Water is part of our daily lives. It is in our food, in the air we breathe and is an essential part of our environment. Water is just as important to other animals and plants. By studying the ways that living organisms make use of this valuable resource scientists may be able to make further improvements to our quality of life.

Glossary

adaptation a change in response to the environment.

aquifer a rock capable of bearing water.

artery large blood vessel with thick muscular walls, leading away from the heart.

atom the smallest particle of any chemical element that can exist alone.

blood a thick, sticky liquid flowing in blood vessels, consisting of cells suspended in plasma.

desalination the removal of salt from sea water.

diffusion the movement of molecules from an area where they are in high concentration to one where they are in lower concentration.

evaporation a change in state from liquid to gas.

excretion the removal of toxic waste products from a living organism.

filtration the separation of particles of one size from other, larger particles.

heat capacity the amount of heat energy required to raise a certain amount of water by one °C.

hormone a chemical messenger found in living organisms.

hydraulic system a system of transmitting forces from one place to another, through a liquid.

irrigation the watering of crops by artificial means.

molecule a group of atoms bonded together.

osmoregulation the control of the amount of water in a living organism.

osmosis the movement of water molecules from a place where they are in high concentration to one where they are lower in concentration through a partially permeable membrane.

purification the cleansing of a substance of impurities.

reservoir a large store of water, often formed by damming a river.

saturation the point at which no more of a substance will dissolve in a solvent.

solute a substance that will dissolve in a solvent.

solvent a substance such as water in which another substance will dissolve.

surface tension a molecular force that pulls the surface of a liquid into the minimum area possible.

sweating the evaporation of sweat (consisting of water, urea and salts) from the surface of the skin.

tissue a group of similar cells with a particular function, for example liver or muscle tissue.

transpiration the evaporation of water from a plant, mostly from the leaves.

water a colourless, odourless liquid made of hydrogen and oxygen.

xerophyte a plant that is adapted to growing in dry conditions, for example a cactus.

Index